Amazing Histories

THE AMAZING HISTORY OF
FOOD

BY KESHA GRANT

CAPSTONE PRESS
a capstone imprint

Published by Capstone Press, an imprint of Capstone.
1710 Roe Crest Drive, North Mankato, Minnesota 56003
capstonepub.com

Library of Congress Cataloging-in-Publication Data is available on the Library of Congress website.
ISBN: 9781669011880 (hardcover)
ISBN: 9781669011835 (paperback)
ISBN: 9781669011842 (ebook PDF)

Summary: How we cook and eat today looks a lot different than it did in the past. From prehistoric kitchens to food preservation and the invention of the refrigerator, the history of food is surprising, unusual, and amazing. Learn more about how people used these innovations to survive and thrive in everyday life.

Editorial Credits
Editor: Alison Deering; Designer: Jaime Willems; Media Researcher: Jo Miller;
Production Specialist: Tori Abraham

Image Credits
Alamy: incamerastock, 17, Old Books Images, 11, World History Archive, 8; Getty Images: Artemidovna, 19, CHUNYIP WONG, 14-15, mikroman6, 7; Newscom: Photoshot, 25; Shutterstock: anitasstudio, 9, Brent Hofacker, 12, CATNIP.films, cover middle, David Orcea, 16, Everett Collection, 20, Georgios Tsichlis, 13, inigolai-Photography, cover right, Ju PhotoStocker, 28, Ken Wolter, 24, Ljupco Smokovski, 5, LumenSt, 10, MAHATHIR MOHD YASIN, 21, Marzolino, cover left, NinaM, 4, NinaM, 6, NinaM, 18, NinaM, 22, 26, 29, Salvador Aznar, 23, silverkblackstock, 27, xMarshall, cover top left,

Printed and bound in the USA. PO 5195

TABLE OF CONTENTS

Words in **BOLD** are in the glossary.

WHAT'S ON
THE MENU?

What do you grab when it's time to snack? Potato chips? A piece of fruit? No matter what you eat, the history of food likely played a part.

PREHISTORIC
KITCHENS

Thousands of years ago, people ate whatever they could find. That included roots, nuts, and berries. They also hunted animals for meat.

People made tools to help them grow plants, hunt, and prepare food. Nets, plows, stone axes, and spears all came in handy.

Artwork shows early humans used tools to cook.

ANCIENT
TIMES

Ancient Egyptians lived along the Nile River. That made it easy for them to get fish. They often broiled or roasted fish over the fire. They also boiled and dried it.

Artwork shows ancient Egyptians fishing along the Nile River.

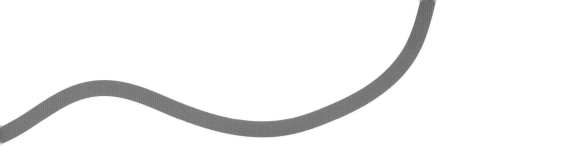

People also ate sweet cakes. Bakers used dates to sweeten more than 40 different kinds of breads and **pastries**.

dates

Ancient India

Spices were popular in India. Cinnamon, salt, and pepper were used to season and **preserve** food. They were also used to make medicines and **incense**.

Spices are used in many different ways in India.

Spices were sold as far away as Japan and Europe. The spice trade lasted for thousands of years.

A busy spice market in Dehli, India

Ancient Greece

The ancient Greeks used olive oil to flavor foods. They also used it to fuel lamps.

DID YOU KNOW?

Ancient Greeks dribbled olive oil onto their skin instead of soap. Then they used wooden tools to scrape away oil, sweat, and dirt.

Each year, farmers harvested thousands of olive trees. The olives were pressed into oil. Oil was then drizzled over food. People dug in with their bare hands!

A farmer holds freshly picked olives in Greece.

Ancient China

To make it easier to get fresh seafood, the ancient Chinese created the world's first "fish farms." These farms raised fish called carp.

A fish pond near a village in Hong Kong

Ancient Hawaiians used these farms too. They herded fish into island "ponds." When the ocean was too rough for fishing, these fish farms kept people fed.

MIDDLE AGES

Today salt is easy to get. But that wasn't always the case. African kingdoms once fought for control over salt. This everyday item was very valuable. It was sometimes traded for gold dust, pound for pound. Salt was literally worth its weight in gold!

DID YOU KNOW?

Mansa Musa, the richest man who ever lived, ruled the kingdom of Mali in Africa. He controlled both the gold and salt trades. In today's dollars, he'd be worth $400 billion.

Food Preservation

Don't like eating fresh fruits and veggies? You're not alone! Some Europeans thought uncooked fruits and vegetables caused disease. They **pickled** these items in jars filled with spices. The jars were stored in chilly basements. In the cold, foods stayed fresher longer.

MODERN
ADVANCES

Ever poured milk over your favorite cereal?
Remember to thank Louis Pasteur. In 1862,
he discovered **pasteurization**. This process
kills harmful germs in dairy products.

Louis Pasteur

Before this, thousands of people died each year of diseases caused by **bacteria** in food. Today, we use this process on fruit juice too.

Refrigeration

By the 1840s, one invention changed how people ate. Refrigerated railroad cars made it possible to move food across long distances. People who didn't have a lot of fresh foods could now enjoy them too.

A worker loads fruit onto a refrigerated truck.

Refrigeration also made it possible to store fresh food longer. This led to less food waste and healthier diets.

The Rise of Fast Food

In 1921, White Castle opened its doors. It was the first fast food chain in the United States. People loved the fast, juicy burgers. They sold for only five cents!

DID YOU KNOW?

Fast food is very popular. In 2021, fast food restaurants in the U.S. earned more than $278 billion.

Customers wait outside a McDonald's in the 1950s.

The first McDonald's opened in 1940.

More fast-food joints soon followed:

1948—In-N-Out opens in California.

1954—Burger King opens in Florida.

1958—Pizza Hut opens in Kansas.

1962—Taco Bell opens in California.

CHANGING
DIETS

In the 1970s, some people were fed up with fast food. Processed foods didn't taste as good as fresh foods. People started a movement called farm to table. It encourages serving local, **organic** food.

Today, farm to table is still popular. Farmers and chefs often work together to bring fresh foods to diners.

Future of Food

What will the food of the future look like? By 2050, there could be nearly 10 billion people on the planet.

A scientist studies crops in a greenhouse.

To feed so many people, scientists are changing the foods we eat. They use science to change the **genes** of **crops**. This helps plants grow faster, fight off diseases, and be more **nutritious**.

GLOSSARY

ancient (AYN-shunt)—from a long time ago

bacteria (bak-TEER-ee-uh)—one-celled, tiny living things; some are helpful and some cause disease

crop (KROP)—a plant farmers grow in large amounts, usually for food

gene (JEEN)—a part of every cell that carries physical and behavioral information

incense (IN-sens)—material used to produce a strong and pleasant smell when burned

nutritious (noo-TRISH-uhss)—containing elements the body uses to stay strong and healthy

organic (or-GAN-ik)—using only natural products and no chemicals or pesticides

pasteurization (pas-tyur-ih-ZAY-shun)—heating process for killing harmful microbes in milk and some other liquids

pastry (PAY-stree)—a sweet baked good, such as pie, made mainly of flour and fat

pickle (PIK-uhl)—to soak or keep in a solution of salt water or vinegar

preserve (pri-ZURV)—to prepare (by canning or pickling) fruits or vegetables to be kept for future use

READ MORE

DK. *The Story of Food: An Illustrated History of Everything We Eat.*
New York: DK Publishing, 2018.

Kenney, Karen Latchana. *Cutting-Edge 3D Printing.* Minneapolis:
Lerner Publishing Group, Inc., 2018.

Kurtz, Kevin. *The Future of Food.* Minneapolis: Lerner Publishing
Group, Inc., 2021.

INTERNET SITES

Easy Science for Kids: History of Food
easyscienceforkids.com/history-of-food

History for Kids
historyforkids.net

National Geographic Kids: Chew on This
kids.nationalgeographic.com/chew-on-this

INDEX

ABOUT THE AUTHOR

photo credit: Malcom Grant

Kesha Grant is an educator, researcher, and children's book author. Her first book, *Women in the Civil Rights Movement: A Scholastic True Book*, was released in 2020. She holds a master's degree in education and a Master of Fine Arts degree in creative writing. She blends these two specialties together to write true accounts of unsung heroes whose stories never made it into the history books but definitely deserve to be there. She lives in Atlanta, Georgia, with her husband, children, and two very fat guinea pigs named Zuko and Boba.